W9-DAF-436

Vermont
impressions

photography by Jim Westphalen

FARCOUNTRY
PRESS

Right: The corn grows tall near Lower Plain.

Title page: Autumn at Smugglers' Notch, a narrow pass used in the nineteenth century for smuggling embargoed goods to Canada.

Front cover: A Cabot farm framed in classic New England fall colors.

Back cover: Elegant Moss Glen Falls, north of Stowe.

ISBN 1-56037-284-2
Photographs © 2004 Jim Westphalen
© 2004 Farcountry Press

This book may not be reproduced in whole or in part by any means (with the exception of short quotes for the purpose of review) without the permission of the publisher. For more information on our books write Farcountry Press, P.O. Box 5630, Helena, MT 59604; call (800) 821-3874; or visit www.farcountrypress.com

Created, produced, and designed in the United States.
Printed in China.

Above: After a process of boiling and filtering, the sap of the maple tree is transformed into delectable syrup.

Facing page: Maple trees tapped with spiles deposit their crystalline sap into awaiting pails.

Following pages: Named after French explorer Samuel de Champlain, Lake Champlain was the site of many military conflicts, including the French and Indian Wars and the American Revolution.

Above: Holsteins near Charlotte.

Right: Enjoying a warm spring day in a Peacham pasture.

Above: Wintry woodlands encased in ice.

Facing page: A stand of birch trees near Underhill scatters its golden foliage to the forest floor.

Following pages: Maples in various stages of seasonal transformation, Greensboro.

Above: Ferns and saplings capture the few rays of sun that pass through the canopy of this wet woodland near Peacham.

Right: This lone maple near Dummerston welcomes spring with its bright new buds.

Above: The stunning view from Devils Hill, near Peacham.

Left: This old Gorhamtown house slowly succumbs to time and ever-encroaching vines of wild cucumber.

Following pages: Day's end in wintry Stowe.

Above: Bingham Waterfall cuts a quiet and delicate path through the woods near Stowe.

Right: The West River flows slowly by the charming village of Weston.

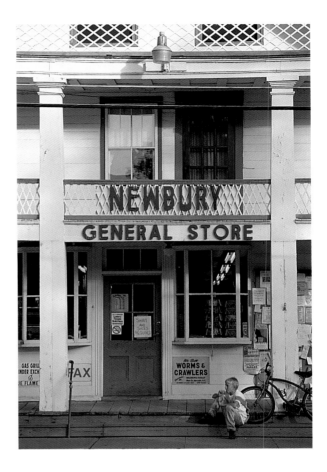

Above: The historic 1840 Newbury General Store, Newbury.

Left: An old Tunbridge farm aglow with the light of early evening.

Following pages: Grayed with age, this wise old barn stands proudly on a Lyndonville farm.

Above: Lake Salem, frozen and asleep
under a heavy blanket of snow.

Right: Back road through fall foliage,
near Corinth Corners.

Above: A heavy fog moves into Shelburne Bay, Lake Champlain.

Left: A quiet Stockbridge farm graces the banks of the White River.

Following pages: The serenity of day's end on a farm nestled in the Green Mountains near Fletcher.

Above: The vista from Mt. Philo offers broad views of Lake Champlain and the Adirondack Mountains beyond.

Left: Richmond's Round Church, actually a sixteen-sided polygon, was constructed in 1813 to serve the city's five Protestant congregations and is now on the National Register of Historic Places.

Above: Jersey cattle, a breed first developed on the island of Jersey in the English Channel, were first brought to the United States in the 1850s.

Right: The Fairfield Country Store, doing business since the 1830s.

Facing page: A Charlotte farm on Lake Champlain.

Above: Picturesque Beebe Pond, in Sunderland.

Left: Hollister Hill Farm, Marshfield.

Following pages: Dusted with snow, Mt. Mansfield—Vermont's highest peak, at 4,393 feet—serves as a reminder that winter will soon come to the valley.

Above: Sailboats ply the calm waters of Lake Dunmore.

Facing page: Stream near East Middlebury follows its
wintry path through a frigid forest.

Above: Fall color underfoot.

Right: This rock wall on Putney Mountain is
one of many created in the eighteenth century
to keep animals off of farmland.

Above: Sheep greet the frigid morning on a Montgomery farm.

Left: A crisp winter evening on an East Berkshire farm.

Following pages: The quiet burg of South Royalton, nestled amid a patchwork of autumn foliage.

Above: Tunbridge farm.

Facing page: The 57-foot-high, Greek Revival–style capitol in Montpelier is crowned with a statue of "Agriculture" and a dome covered in 23.7-carat gold leaf.

Above: Fishing the White River as it reflects
a fiery sunset, near Royalton.

Right: Farm atop a bluff near New Haven.

Above: Scenic Holland Pond is home to many species of wildlife, including great blue herons, river otters, ospreys, and moose.

Left: The 1859 Shelburne Country Store in Shelburne.

Facing page: The Lapointe Sugarhouse, cooking up sweet concoctions deep in the woods near Craftsbury.

Following pages: West branch of the Waterbury River, near Stowe.

Above: Placid Emerald Lake, headwaters of Otter Creek.

Facing page: This verdant pastoral scene near Tunbridge
recalls another century.

Above: Marshfield Pond.

Left: The village of East Corinth is nestled between Sleeper Hill and McArthur Hill.

Following pages: The dense woodlands of Hazen's Notch.

Above: Hiking a winter wonderland on the summit of Mt. Mansfield.

Right: Farm along the fertile banks of the mirror-like Winooski River.

Above: Curious lambs wander in for a close-up, Westminster West.

Facing page: Friendly porch in Bristol. Folks in this small town of less than 4,000 celebrate the Fourth of July every year with a festival and parade, the longest-running parade in Vermont.

Above: Trees cast their adornments at the foot of modest Middletown Springs Congregational Church, built in 1796.

Right: Moonrise on a Cornwall farm.

Above: Plant life thrives in the marshes near Ferrisburg.

Left: Mount Mansfield is shrouded in early morning fog near Cambridge.

Following pages: Scenic byway snakes through historic Smugglers' Notch.

Above: A kayaker negotiates the rapids on the scenic White River.

Left: Sunset tinges pink this wintry scene near Charlotte.

Above: The charming 1852 West Arlington Covered Bridge is one of several covered bridges that span the Battenkill River.

Right: Chandler Pond, in South Wheelock, reflects the vivid palette of the forest that surrounds it.

Above: Spring pond, Weston.

Left: An approaching spring storm threatens this vibrant valley near Waterbury Center.

Following pages: A pleasing rural panorama, near Fairfax.

© Kendra Dew

JIM WESTPHALEN

Jim has been a commercial and fine-art photographer for more than twenty years. His work has been published widely in advertisements, magazines, and calendars nationally and abroad and is shown in numerous galleries throughout the state of Vermont.

Motivated by the natural beauty and mystique of New England, Jim moved in 1996 from his home on Long Island, N.Y., to Vermont, where he now runs a successful studio. Though he spends much of his time on commercial assignments, his first love and inspiration is photographing the timeless Vermont landscape.

The collection of images in this book represents Jim's first six years living in and photographing Vermont and expresses his passion for the place he now calls home.

www.jimwestphalen.com